D0383102

FALAFEL FOREVER

FALAFEL FOREVER

Nutritious and tasty recipes for fried, baked, raw, vegan and more!

DUNJA GULIN

photography by Tim Atkins

LONDON • NEW YORK

Senior Designer Megan Smith
Editors Kate Eddison and
   Alice Sambrook
Production Mai-Ling Collyer
Art Director Leslie Harrington
Editorial Director Julia Charles
Publisher Cindy Richards

Food Stylist Emily Kydd
Prop Stylist Jenny Iggleden
Indexer Vanessa Bird

First published in 2017 by
Ryland Peters & Small
20–21 Jockey's Fields
London WC1R 4BW,
and 341 E 116th St,
New York, NY 10029
www.rylandpeters.com

10 9 8 7 6 5 4 3 2 1

Text © Dunja Gulin 2017
Design and photographs
© Ryland Peters & Small 2017
All photography by Tim Atkins
except page 13 by Mowie Kay

ISBN: 978-1-84975-816-1

Printed in China

The author's moral rights have been
asserted. All rights reserved. No part
of this publication may be reproduced,
stored in a retrieval system or
transmitted in any form or by any
means, electronic, mechanical,
photocopying or otherwise, without
the prior permission of the publisher.

A CIP record for this book is available
from the British Library. US Library of
Congress cataloging-in-publication
data has been applied for.

Dedication
To my grandmas
Milena and Fumica

CONTENTS

Introduction   6

Tips and tricks   8

Fried   10

Baked   26

Raw   34

Meals   44

Sauces and dips   52

Index   62

Cook's notes   64

INTRODUCTION

Growing up, I'd never heard of falafel, let alone eaten it or seen it being prepared – it's not something you would find on the streets of the small town in Istria, Croatia, where I was raised in the 1980s. However, all the ingredients were readily available and could be frequently found in the kitchens of my grandmas and my parents; chickpeas/garbanzo beans were a staple, especially in stews and for salads. Actually, my grandma has been cultivating chickpeas/garbanzo beans since the 1960s and, even today, each time I visit her I know that a huge bag of them will be waiting for me on my way out!

It wasn't until the late 1990s, when I moved to London as a young foodie on a mission to discover new tastes, that I first saw and tasted falafel. I clearly remember that Saturday in Shepherd's Bush Market when a falafel stall caught my attention. I had no smartphone to take me to a good vegetarian restaurant and there were no website reviews telling me what's tasty and what's not – looking for food in a big city was a totally different experience back then! I asked the vendor a couple of questions, and as soon as I heard the word 'chickpeas' I knew that was it! The wrap I bought was like nothing I had tasted before – warm fritters wrapped in pitta bread with just the right balance of creaminess and tanginess from the hummus and the pickles and the added veggies. Wow! It wasn't long before I copied a falafel recipe from a Middle Eastern cookbook in a bookstore, and I have been making my own falafel ever since!

My grandma's chickpeas/garbanzo beans are still the most important ingredient to me when making falafel. However, over time, I have experimented with many other ingredients that can be used to make alternative falafel-like dishes. This means that people who don't like fried foods, or who find traditional falafel difficult to digest, or even those who are following a raw food diet, don't have to miss out on enjoying a good falafel-like meal!

I sincerely hope you will like my selection of fried, baked and raw falafels. They are all vegan, packed with nutrients and, hopefully, full of deliciousness! Enjoy!

TIPS AND TRICKS

I make all kinds of falafels, and I find that when people try them or see a photo the questions usually start popping up: How come they aren't falling apart or soaking up all the oil? How do I achieve the fine crust and the juicy inside? What is the secret ingredient that makes them so tasty? These, along with many other questions, reveals that making really good falafel can be a tricky business. Now that I think of it, there are a couple of crucial moments where a small mistake can make the difference between a perfect falafel and a falafel mix that ends up being thrown away! So, dear foodie friends, it is my duty to reveal all my tips and tricks, and I sincerely hope you find these instructions helpful!

- When making falafel with soaked chickpeas/garbanzo beans, make sure they are soaked for at least 24 hours. Not only will the 24-hour soak make them softer and easier to blend, but the falafel will be easier to digest and you'll feel lighter and more nourished after a falafel meal.
- When making cooked grain-based and bean-based falafel, if using leftover grains and beans, make sure they are at room temperature, not fridge-cold.
- When vegetables are part of the falafel mix, chop them or grate them finely. Otherwise, bigger pieces might cause the mix to fall apart during frying.
- Mix well, or even knead the falafel mixture for a while, until all the ingredients are well combined.

- Never use bread crumbs to bind the mixture if it seems wet – your falafel will fall apart and soak up loads of oil. This rule is for deep-fried falafel only; for shallow-frying or baking, adding bread crumbs to the mix is totally okay.
- Most falafel mixes have to sit for at least half an hour to bind well.
- Use a small heavy-bottom stainless-steel or cast-iron pan/skillet for frying.
- Falafels made from soaked chickpeas or lentils need to fry for longer than falafels made from cooked grains or beans in order to be cooked properly.
- Add enough oil to the pan for deep-frying (at least three fingers up from the bottom of the saucepan).
- Heat the oil until it starts 'moving' – the right temperature of the frying oil is really important. If the oil isn't hot enough, the falafel will sink, soak up loads of oil and start falling apart. If, on the other hand, the oil is too hot, the falafel will burn from the outside and stay uncooked on the inside.
- Once you place a couple of falafels in the pan, the oil should immediately sizzle and foam. If this does not happen, you need to preheat the oil a bit more.
- Overcrowding the pan will result in a dramatic drop in oil temperature and this will cause the falafel to fall apart and/or turn oily and uncooked. How many to cook at once depends on the size of your pan, but there should always be some free space left.

- If you're making a big batch of falafels that are rolled into flour or seeds, you'll probably, at some point, need to filter the oil through a steel sieve/strainer to remove burnt flour and food particles. These would, otherwise, spoil the taste and make the last batch taste bitter and burnt.
- Once the falafels are well browned (it is especially important to well-fry falafels that are made with soaked beans), use a skimmer to take them out and place them on a paper towel-lined plate. The oil mark on the towel should be small and not widely spread around your falafel. They should be compact, with a thin crust and a juicy inside, and should only lightly grease your fingers.
- Ready falafel mix made with soaked chickpeas/garbanzo beans can be frozen, and so can formed, uncooked falafel and already-fried leftover falafel. My advice is to fry the entire amount, and then freeze the leftovers. This way you only need to defrost them, drizzle some oil over and bake in the oven until crispy. They taste almost better than freshly fried falafel!

Surely you have tasted, or maybe even prepared, one version of this classic falafel recipe. An intensive 24-hour soak makes the chickpeas properly soft, which gives a lovely moist yet light mixture that is easy to digest.

TRADITIONAL CHICKPEA FALAFEL POCKETS

180 g/1 cup dried
    chickpeas/garbanzo
    beans
80 g/⅔ cup chopped
    onion
2 garlic cloves
1 bunch fresh parsley,
    leaves only
2 teaspoons ground
    coriander
½ teaspoon bicarbonate
    of soda/baking soda
1 teaspoon ground cumin
⅛ teaspoon chilli/chili
    powder
1½ teaspoons salt
230 ml/1 cup oil, for frying

SERVING SUGGESTION
4 pitta pockets
Tahini Sauce (see page 58)
raw vegetables (such as
    sliced tomatoes,
    cucumber, lettuce,
    rocket/arugula, parsley,
    spring onions/scallions)

MAKES 24-26 SMALL FALAFELS

Soak the chickpeas/garbanzo beans in plenty of water for 12 hours. Drain, discarding the water, cover with fresh water and let soak for another 12 hours. Drain, rinse well and let drain again for another 5 minutes.

It's best to use a food processor fitted with an 'S' blade for blending the falafel mix, even though it can also be done in a good blender, in two batches.

First blend the drained chickpeas/garbanzo beans; the texture should resemble coarse sand. Add all the remaining ingredients (except the frying oil) and blend until you get a paste. Cover with clingfilm/plastic wrap and let sit in the fridge for 1 hour, or longer.

Roll into walnut-sized balls, wetting your hands once in a while to prevent sticking.

Deep-fry the falafels in hot oil for 4 minutes or until nicely browned (see tips page 8). Because we're using soaked chickpeas/garbanzo beans, these falafels need to be deep-fried to make them digestible – baking them wouldn't work.

Warm the pitta pockets, fill with vegetables of your choice, add falafel balls and serve with the tahini sauce. Yum!

The most important step in making this falafel is to blend all the ingredients really well into a thick paste. Chunky falafel mix burns easily and tends to fall apart during frying – we want these pointed falafels to get a nice crunchy crust with a juicy, bright-green inside. You can use fresh or thawed peas instead of broad/fava beans, with equally yummy results.

FRESH BROAD/FAVA BEAN FALAFEL

350 g/2⅓ cups shelled
    fresh broad/fava beans
2 garlic cloves, crushed
½ small bunch fresh mint,
    leaves only
½ small bunch fresh
    parsley, leaves only
½ teaspoon salt
¼ teaspoon cumin seeds,
    crushed
1 teaspoon ground
    coriander
1 tablespoon gram flour
    (chickpea/garbanzo
    bean flour)
230 ml/1 cup oil, for frying

SERVING SUGGESTION
baked pumpkin squares
pink or regular sauerkraut
rocket/arugula or
    microgreens
Cashew Yogurt Sauce or
    Tofu Mayonnaise
    (see page 53)

MAKES 10 FALAFELS

Bring a pan of water to the boil and boil the broad/fava beans for 1 minute. Drain and run them under cold water to cool them down to the point where you can handle them. Pinch their skins off with your fingers and slip the inner bright green bean out. You should get about 250 g/1½ cups peeled beans.

In a food processor fitted with an 'S' blade, chop the mint and parsley, then add the skinned beans and whiz until chopped into a paste. Scoop into a bowl, add the remaining ingredients (except the frying oil) and knead for a second to incorporate.

Scoop up a small amount of mixture and use two spoons to shape into oval balls with lightly pointed ends. Deep-fry in hot oil for 3–4 minutes or until nicely browned (see tips page 8).

I serve these falafels in wide bowls, placed alongside baked pumpkin, pink sauerkraut and rocket/arugula, and drizzled with cashew sauce or tofu mayo. A very satisfying and nutritious meal!

Chickpeas/garbanzo beans aren't the only legumes you can soak to make falafel! Red lentils are also an option – they make a falafel that is softer and easier to digest, and the soaking time is shorter! I usually add Indian spices to the mix, as well as young chard greens from my garden, but feel free to use any spices and any type of soft greens you can lay your hands on!

RED LENTIL FALAFEL WRAPS

- 90 g/½ cup split red lentils
- 40 g/1 cup finely chopped chard or spinach
- 2 garlic cloves
- ½ teaspoon salt
- 1 teaspoon finely chopped fresh ginger
- 1 teaspoon curry powder
- ½ teaspoon ground coriander
- ½ teaspoon ground turmeric
- ½ teaspoon garam masala
- ½ teaspoon ground ginger
- ⅛ teaspoon chilli/chili powder (or to taste)
- 230 ml/1 cup oil, for frying

SERVING SUGGESTION
wholegrain tortillas
young lettuce leaves
Super Simple Salsa
  (see page 54)
Herb and Avocado Dip
  (see page 54)

MAKES 12 FALAFELS

Wash the red lentils thoroughly and let soak in plenty of water overnight. Drain, rinse well and let drain again for 5 minutes. It's best to use a food processor fitted with an 'S' blade for blending the falafel mix, even though it can also be done in a good blender. Blend all the ingredients (except the frying oil) until you get a paste – the texture should resemble coarse sand.

Roll into walnut-sized balls, then pat them down just a little to get chubby oval-shaped falafels. To prevent sticking, wet your hands while shaping.

Deep-fry the falafels in hot oil for 4 minutes or until nicely browned (see tips page 8). Because we're using soaked lentils, these falafels need to be deep-fried to make them digestible – baking them wouldn't work.

To assemble, warm the tortillas in the oven, add some lettuce and 4 or 5 falafels on top of each one, together with two tablespoons each of salsa and avocado dip. Wrap up and serve with extra dips. Or, even better, put all the ingredients on the table and let everyone make their own wraps!

This is a falafel recipe with a slightly different spice twist! The fennel taste from the seeds and the bulb itself pair well with the refreshing citrus aroma from the lemon zest. A must try!

FENNEL AND LEMON-SCENTED FALAFEL

180 g/1 cup dried
  chickpeas/garbanzo
  beans
2 shallots
2 garlic cloves
½ bunch fresh fennel
  fronds or coriander/
  cilantro leaves
1 teaspoon fennel seeds,
  crushed
1 teaspoon grated lemon
  zest (from organic
  lemons)
½ teaspoon bicarbonate
  of soda/baking soda
1 teaspoon ground
  coriander
⅛ teaspoon chilli/chili
  powder
1½ teaspoons salt
230 ml/1 cup oil, for frying

SERVING SUGGESTION
pitta pockets
Romaine lettuce leaves
fennel bulb, shaved into
  thin shavings using a
  vegetable peeler
pickles
Tahini Sauce (see page 58,
  or other sauce of choice)
lemon wedges

MAKES 24-26 SMALL FALAFELS

Soak the chickpeas/garbanzo beans in plenty of water for 12 hours. Drain, discarding the water, cover with fresh water and let soak for another 12 hours. Drain, rinse well and let drain again for another 5 minutes. The 24-hour soak will make the falafel easier to digest and the mixture won't be too dry.

It's best to use a food processor fitted with an 'S' blade for blending the falafel mix, even though it can also be done in a good blender, in two batches.

First blend the drained chickpeas/garbanzo beans, the texture should resemble coarse sand. Add all the remaining ingredients (except the frying oil) and blend until you get a paste. Cover with clingfilm/plastic wrap and let sit in the fridge for 1 hour, or longer.

Roll into walnut-sized balls, wetting your hands once in a while to prevent sticking. Deep-fry the falafels in hot oil for 4 minutes or until nicely browned (see tips page 8). Because we're using soaked chickpeas/garbanzo beans, these falafels need to be deep-fried to make them digestible – baking them wouldn't work.

Warm the pitta pockets and fill them with lettuce, fennel shavings, pickles and falafel balls and serve with tahini sauce and lemon wedges.

If you're looking for an instant falafel recipe that requires minimal prep, check out these crunchy beauties! Serving them with a fair amount of sauce is key, since the use of gram flour (chickpea/garbanzo bean flour), instead of soaked chickpeas/garbanzo beans, results in a slightly drier consistency.

CHICKPEA FLOUR AND HARISSA PATTIES

120 g/1 cup gram flour
(chickpea/garbanzo
bean flour)
¼ teaspoon bicarbonate
of soda/baking soda
½ teaspoon salt
½ teaspoon ground
coriander
1 teaspoon harissa powder
(or to taste)
¼ teaspoon dried oregano
30 g/1 tablespoon very
finely chopped onion
80 ml/⅓ cup hot water
3 tablespoons coconut oil
(or other oil), for frying
harissa paste and Tofu
Mayonnaise (see page
53), to serve (optional)

MAKES 8-10 PATTIES

Combine the flour with the other dry ingredients, mix in the chopped onion and slowly start incorporating the hot water. You should get a non-sticky dough that can be shaped easily. Let the mixture sit for 10 minutes before forming it into small patties.

Heat the oil in a non-stick frying pan/skillet over medium heat. Depending on the size of your pan you will need to fry them in at least two batches. Make sure not to overcrowd the pan. Lower the heat and let the falafels fry for 3–4 minutes on each side, or until golden brown. If you wish to build your spicy food tolerance, serve these with plenty of harissa paste, as well as tofu mayonnaise to cool!

I love tempeh, but it took me years to realize that the texture of it, when mashed, is absolutely perfect for falafel-style recipes! It binds together so well and doesn't absorb any oil during frying, which is kind of a big deal! Chilli flakes/hot pepper flakes add spiciness, and Kala Namak gives a very light egg-like aroma that non-vegans will appreciate.

ROBUST TEMPEH FAUX-LAFEL

300 g/2½ cups tempeh
70 g/½ cup finely chopped green (bell) pepper
3 tablespoons freshly chopped parsley or coriander/cilantro leaves
1 garlic clove, crushed
½ teaspoon isot Kurdish black pepper flakes (or other chilli flakes/ hot pepper flakes)
¾ teaspoon Kala Namak (black salt powder)
230 ml/1 cup oil, for frying

MAKES 10 LARGE OR 20 SMALL FALAFELS

Cover the whole piece of tempeh with boiling water in a pan and simmer for 15 minutes. This will make the tempeh softer, easier to digest and the falafel won't crumble (but you can skip cooking the tempeh if you're in a hurry). Drain, let cool a little, then mash with a fork.

Add all the other ingredients (except the frying oil) and mix well, preferably with your hands, to form a compact dough.

Form the mixture into falafels (either 10 large ones or 20 small ones) and deep-fry in hot oil for 2–3 minutes or until golden brown (see tips page 8).

My favourite ways to serve these include: with pasta and tomato sauce in winter; or with vegan mayo, fresh tomato salsa and sliced avocado in summer.

How 'Greek-style' this courgette/zucchini falafel actually is I have no idea, but the courgette/zucchini base, the chickpea/garbanzo bean addition and the yogurt-cucumber serving sauce made me think of one hot summer I spent in Greece a long time ago, enjoying amazing home-cooked food!

GREEK-STYLE FALAFEL FRITTERS

560 g/4 cups grated courgette/zucchini
1 teaspoon salt, plus extra to taste
4 tablespoons freshly chopped parsley leaves
¼ teaspoon ground turmeric
¼ teaspoon ground cumin
½ teaspoon ground coriander
80 g/½ cup gram flour (chickpea/garbanzo bean flour)
freshly ground black pepper
olive oil, for shallow-frying

SERVING SUGGESTION
Tzatziki Sauce
   (see page 61)
lemon wedges
freshly chopped
   coriander/cilantro
flatbreads

MAKES 14-16 FRITTERS

Put the grated courgette/zucchini in a bowl, add the 1 teaspoon salt, mix well and let sit for 10 minutes. Squeeze out most of the courgette/zucchini juice and discard. Add the parsley, turmeric, cumin, coriander, flour, pepper and more salt to taste, then quickly mix with a spatula.

With the help of a small round cookie cutter or a measuring tablespoon, form 14–16 even-sized patties and flatten them down a bit.

Heat a non-stick frying pan/skillet over medium heat, add a little olive oil and fry the falafels for 3–4 minutes on each side until golden brown. Serve with tzatziki sauce, lemon wedges, coriander/cilantro and flatbreads, or whichever way you like!

These falafels are crunchy on the outside and creamy on the inside, but make sure to serve them freshly fried! Kalamata olives can be omitted entirely or substituted with other types of olives, or even with chopped corn kernels, especially in summer. Tofu is rich in plant protein, has a mild taste and is an excellent occasional food for those of us who prefer plant-based meals that are light, yet nourishing.

CRUNCHY TOFU FAUX-LAFEL

280 g/1½ cups fresh firm tofu
90 g/½ cup Kalamata olives
2 tablespoons freshly chopped coriander/cilantro leaves or snipped chives
2 tablespoons gram flour (chickpea/garbanzo bean flour)
½ teaspoon ground turmeric
freshly ground black pepper
salt, if needed
230 ml/1 cup oil, for frying

SERVING SUGGESTION
roasted vegetables of your choice
vegan mayo or good-quality ketchup

MAKES 16-18 FALAFELS

In a food processor fitted with an 'S' blade, process the tofu until creamy. Transfer it into a mixing bowl.

Drain, pat dry and finely chop the Kalamata olives and add them to the tofu with coriander/cilantro or chives, gram flour (chickpea/garbanzo bean flour), turmeric, pepper and salt. Combine well with a silicone spatula.

Roll into 16–18 even-sized balls, wetting your hands once in a while to prevent sticking. Deep-fry the falafels in hot oil for 2–3 minutes or until golden brown (see tips page 8).

Serve hot or warm with plenty of veggies, cooked and raw and with some vegan mayo or good-quality ketchup.

BAKED

These millet-based croquettes still carry the distinct falafel flavour, with an added barbecue kick from the spice mix! Millet is a healthy grain, rich in iron and other nutrients, and if there are some cooked leftovers lying around in my fridge, I often use them to make these elegant croquettes. They are always well received, even by otherwise picky eaters!

BBQ FALAFEL CROQUETTES

100 g/½ cup millet

300 ml/1¼ cups boiling water

2 tablespoons finely chopped onion

1 teaspoon finely chopped garlic

1 teaspoon ground coriander

1½ teaspoons barbecue spice rub (with added salt)

6 g/¼ cup freshly chopped parsley leaves

80 g/¼ cup dry polenta

olive oil, for brushing

baking sheet, lined with baking parchment

MAKES 10 CROQUETTES

Wash and drain the millet well, then place in a saucepan and pour over the boiling water. Cover, lower the heat to a minimum and simmer for 12–15 minutes, until the millet soaks up all the liquid and becomes soft. Spread on a plate to cool. (You can also use leftover cooked millet from previous meals, and skip this stage.)

Preheat the oven to 180°C (350°F) Gas 4.

Place the cooked millet in a large bowl and add the onion, garlic, spices and parsley. Knead well into a sticky dough that holds together.

Form 10 cylinder-shaped croquettes, brush each with oil on all sides and roll them in the polenta. Transfer to the lined baking sheet and bake in the preheated oven for 15–20 minutes or until golden brown. They will brown nicely if you switch on the grill/broiler mode at the end of baking. Serve while warm.

This recipe was created in one of those moments when you really fancy a falafel meal but you don't really have the necessary ingredients... So you just take out all the leftovers from the fridge and trust your cooking experience to guide you through the creative process of birthing a new recipe! The result is sometimes, as in this case, a very tasty dish and a real keeper!

CHUNKY BAKED FALAFEL PATTIES

½ large onion
   (about 60 g/2 oz.)
2 garlic cloves
320 g/2 cups cooked red
   kidney beans, well
   drained
2 tablespoons toasted
   ground sesame seeds
   or ground flaxseeds
1 tablespoon dark sesame
   oil (or pumpkin seed oil
   or olive oil)
1 teaspoon salt
2 tablespoons gram flour
   (chickpea/garbanzo
   bean flour)
¼ teaspoon bicarbonate
   of soda/baking soda

SERVING SUGGESTION
toasted sourdough
Roasted Red Pepper and
   Mustard Sauce
   (see page 57)
rocket/arugula
pickled vegetables of
   your choice

*baking sheet, lined with
baking paper*

MAKES 18 PATTIES

Preheat the oven to 180°C (350°F) Gas 4.

In a food processor fitted with an 'S' blade, finely chop the onion and garlic. Mash the beans with a fork, leaving some chunks, then mix the beans with the chopped vegetables and all the other ingredients. The mix should resemble a thick cookie dough. Use a measuring spoon to scoop 18 flat, free-form patties onto the lined baking sheet.

Bake in the preheated oven for 15–20 minutes, until dry enough to separate from the baking sheet without falling apart.

These falafel patties are on the saltier side and I love them served on slices of freshly baked or just toasted sourdough bread with roasted red pepper and mustard sauce, rocket/arugula and any type of pickled vegetables on the side.

You can use cooked chickpeas/garbanzo beans instead of kidney beans for a more authentic falafel flavour, if you like.

Baked falafels are a little drier than falafels which are deep-fried in oil, so I always serve them with some kind of sauce. These are just perfect on whole-wheat pasta with tomato sauce, just like real meatballs!

FALAFEL 'MEATBALLS'

320 g/2 cups cooked green or brown lentils, well drained
50 g/½ cup fine rolled oats
70 g/½ cup finely grated carrot or celeriac/celery root (or leftover veggie pulp from juicing)
2 garlic cloves, crushed
1 teaspoon dried oregano
½ teaspoon salt
4 tablespoons unbleached flour, for rolling
oil, for greasing and brushing

SERVING SUGGESTION
cooked whole-wheat or white spaghetti
fresh tomato sauce

baking sheet, lined with baking paper

MAKES 12 FALAFELS

Mix together all the ingredients (except the flour and oil) in a bowl and let sit in the fridge for at least 1 hour, or overnight.

Preheat the oven to 180°C (350°F) Gas 4.

Form the mixture into walnut-sized balls, flatten them slightly and roll in flour, shaking off any excess flour.

Grease the baking paper with oil and oil each falafel with the help of a silicone brush when you place them on the baking sheet.

Bake in the preheated oven for 20 minutes; no need for turning them. They are done when a thin crust is formed and they dry out slightly while getting a golden hue. Serve freshly baked, but they taste good served the next day, too.

A very basic recipe made of wholegrains and veggies that can be served even to small children – just reduce the amount of spices!

JUICY BROWN RICE FAUX-LAFEL

420 g/3 cups cooked short-grain brown rice (cooked 2:1 water to rice ratio)

70 g/½ cup very finely grated carrot (about 1 carrot)

40 g/½ cup very finely grated celeriac/celery root

80 g/½ cup very finely grated onion (1 small onion)

4 garlic cloves, crushed

40 g/¼ cup finely grated smoked tofu (optional)

2 tablespoons freshly chopped parsley or spring onion/scallion greens

salt, pepper, oregano, chilli/chili powder and sweet paprika, to taste

olive oil, for greasing and brushing

SERVING SUGGESTION
mixed greens
sauce or dip of your choice (see pages 52–61)

baking sheet, lined with baking paper

MAKES ABOUT 24 SMALL BURGERS

For this dish the rice has to be carefully cooked: it should be neither soggy nor hard. For best results use freshly cooked rice, but if using leftover rice from the fridge, bring to room temperature first.

Put the cooked rice, grated veggies, garlic, tofu, parsley and some salt, pepper, oregano, chilli/chili powder and paprika in a big bowl. Use your hands to knead the mixture until the ingredients are well combined. Taste and add more salt, pepper, oregano, chilli/chili powder or paprika if needed.

Wet your hands and try to shape a small burger from the mixture – if it is a little sticky and soft, but the burger keeps its shape, it should be ready. Leave the mixture to sit in the fridge for 1 hour, or longer.

Preheat the oven to 180°C (350°F) Gas 4.

Wet your hands and shape about 24 small burgers. Grease the baking paper with oil and oil each falafel with the help of a silicone brush when you place them on the baking sheet.

Bake in the preheated oven for 12–16 minutes or until golden and compact, with a thin, crunchy crust and a juicy inside. Depending on the oven, you might want to turn them halfway through baking. These are delicious served on a bed of mixed greens and with a sauce or dip of your choice.

A lot of people love falafels, but don't like deep-fried foods, or have difficulty digesting the soaked chickpeas/garbanzo beans that are usually in falafels. Here's a raw and chickpea-free falafel that is surprisingly easy to make, and will fill you up for many hours! I'm using seeds and herbs that are available to me locally on the Mediterranean coast, but feel free to use what you can find.

MEDITERRANEAN SEED FALAFEL

120 g/1 cup pumpkin seeds
70 g/½ cup sunflower
   seeds
60 g/½ cup walnuts
6 sun-dried tomato
   halves, soaked
50 g/½ cup fresh basil
   leaves
50 g/½ cup fresh parsley
   leaves
½ teaspoon dried oregano
½ teaspoon
   Mediterranean dried
   herbs mix (thyme,
   savory, marjoram,
   rosemary, basil, fennel)
2 garlic cloves, crushed
1–2 tablespoons olive oil
1 tablespoon lemon juice,
   or to taste
salt, to taste

SERVING SUGGESTION
Romaine lettuce leaves
sliced tomato
grated courgettes/
   zucchini and carrots
sliced spring onions/
   scallions
Tahini Sauce (see page 58)

MAKES 10-12 FALAFELS

Grind the seeds and walnuts into fine flour (I have a small electric coffee grinder just for this purpose). Chop the tomatoes very finely. Add the chopped tomatoes, together with the remaining ingredients, to the seed flour and mix well with your hands or with a silicone spatula. Wrap in clingfilm/plastic wrap and let sit in the fridge for 30 minutes. (If you are in a hurry, you can skip the resting time and make them right away.)

Pull off portions of the mixture (about the size of small walnuts) and roll into balls.

To serve, put 2–3 falafels on a Romaine lettuce leaf with some tomato, courgette/zucchini, carrot and spring onions/scallions. Top with a drizzle of the tahini sauce or any sauce of your choosing. Roll up like a wrap and munch away!

As the gluten-free movement spreads around the globe, buckwheat has recently seen a rise in popularity. However, there's more to buckwheat than just the fact that it doesn't contain gluten! Since it's technically not a grain, it's much softer than other grains and I use it soaked to make all kinds of raw dishes, including crackers, flatbreads, custard-like creams and, of course, this falafel-style treat for those who prefer uncooked foods.

BUCKWHEAT AND CAULIFLOWER BITES

80 g/½ cup buckwheat, soaked overnight, drained well
120 g/1 cup cauliflower florets
½ large onion (about 60 g/2 oz.)
4 sun-dried tomato halves (soaked in hot water, or tapped dry if in oil)
1 tablespoon olive oil
3 tablespoons freshly snipped chives or chopped parsley
½ teaspoon dried thyme
¼–½ teaspoon salt

SERVING SUGGESTION
mixed salad
Super Simple Salsa (see page 54)
avocado slices

dehydrator lined with a tex-flex sheet (or a baking sheet lined with baking parchment)

MAKES 18 BITES

In a small food processor fitted with an 'S' blade, blend the soaked buckwheat until sticky but with some texture left. Scoop the buckwheat into a bowl.

Process the cauliflower and add to the buckwheat. Chop the onion and tomato halves and add to the buckwheat mix along with all the other ingredients. Mix with a spatula to incorporate.

Scoop up a small amount of the falafel mixture and use two spoons to shape little oval balls and place them onto the lined dehydrator or baking sheet.

Dehydrate on 60°C (140°F) for 1 hour, lower to 45°C (115°F) and continue dehydrating until the falafels form a crust, with a still slightly moist inside (takes 4–5 additional hours). (Alternatively, use the oven: Turn it to the lowest setting, and put in the baking sheet with falafels, wedging the door open with a rolled-up dish towel to prevent overheating.)

Serve with a big salad, simple salsa and slices of avocado. Or however you may fancy!

This recipe proves that it is worth allowing ourselves to jump out of the box and try different methods of food preparation. Drying on low temperature, instead of regular baking, develops an amazingly aromatic taste, especially in recipes with mushrooms. A great example of how natural ingredients combined with the right spices can result in a delicious and gourmet dish!

MUSHROOM AND WALNUT FALAFEL

60 g/½ cup walnuts
70 g/1 cup chopped fresh shiitake mushrooms (or other)
½ small courgette/zucchini (about 50 g/2 oz.)
1 garlic clove
small bunch fresh parsley, leaves only
½ small onion (about 40 g/1½ oz.)
2 tablespoons ground flaxseeds, or toasted, ground sesame seeds
1 tablespoon tamari soy sauce
1 tablespoon extra virgin olive oil
⅛ teaspoon salt

dash of chilli/chili powder and cinnamon powder
¼ teaspoon ground ginger
1 teaspoon freshly squeezed lemon juice

SERVING SUGGESTION
plain soy yogurt
spiralized raw vegetables
lemon dressing

dehydrator lined with a tex-flex sheet (or a baking sheet lined with baking parchment)

MAKES 14 WALNUT-SIZED FALAFELS

In a food processor fitted with an 'S' blade, separately chop the walnuts, then the mushrooms, then the courgette/zucchini, garlic, parsley leaves and onion.

Mix together in a bowl, then add ground flaxseeds or sesame seeds, soy sauce, oil, salt, spices and lemon juice and combine all the ingredients into a moist paste.

Use a measuring spoon to scoop walnut-sized falafels onto the lined dehydrator or baking sheet.

Dehydrate on 60°C (140°F) for 1 hour, lower to 45°C (115°F) and continue dehydrating until the falafels form a crust, with a still slightly moist inside (takes 4–5 additional hours). (Alternatively, use the oven: Turn it to the lowest setting, and put in the baking sheet with falafels, wedging the door open with a rolled-up dish towel to prevent overheating.)

Because this falafel has a strong flavour, I like to eat it with plain chilled soy yogurt and a big bowl of spiralized raw vegetables drizzled with a light lemon dressing. A perfect light lunch that will nourish you without leaving you feeling heavy!

Another falafel-style recipe with nuts as the main ingredient that can be
dried in the dehydrator or the oven. You can substitute cashews for soaked
sunflower seeds or walnuts, but do not omit the sweet paprika or fresh red
(bell) pepper, as both of these give the distinctive flavour and colour to this
falafel. These will keep well in the fridge and are a great lunchbox item, too.

PAPRIKA AND CASHEW FALAFEL

220 g/2 cups cashews
¼ teaspoon salt,
  for soaking
70 g/½ cup red (bell)
  pepper, seeded and
  chopped
40 g/¼ cup chopped
  onion
3 tablespoons freshly
  chopped parsley leaves
3 teaspoons sweet paprika
½ teaspoon salt
2 tablespoons virgin
  coconut oil, melted

SERVING SUGGESTION
summer salad with baby
  spinach leaves, chopped
  onion and radish
Tahini Sauce (see page 58)
extra seeds, to sprinkle

dehydrator lined with a
tex-flex sheet (or a baking
sheet lined with baking
parchment)

MAKES 18-20 PIECES

Put the cashews in a bowl, cover with water, add
the ¼ teaspoon salt and let soak for 8 hours or
overnight. Discard the soaking water and drain well.

Blend the soaked cashews in a high-speed
blender together with the remaining ingredients
until smooth.

Use a measuring spoon to scoop walnut-sized
falafels onto the lined dehydrator or baking sheet.

Dehydrate on 60°C (140°F) for 1 hour, lower to
45°C (115°F) and continue dehydrating until the
falafels form a crust, with a still slightly moist inside
(takes 4–5 additional hours). (Alternatively, use the
oven: Turn it to the lowest setting, and put in the
baking sheet with falafels, wedging the door open
with a rolled-up dish towel to prevent overheating.)

You'll love this vegetable-rich recipe! Another raw version of healthier falafel bites that will surprise and impress even the most sceptic eaters. These pink falafels are a perfect lunchbox/picnic item, served with Herb and Avocado Dip (see page 54) or hummus, a juicy summer salad of ripe tomatoes, crisp cucumber, leaves and slightly bitter olives. Or, in the winter, pair with a hearty soup for a quick lunch or light dinner.

PINK SUN-SEED FALAFEL

140 g/1 cup sunflower seeds (raw or slightly sprouted)
2 small carrots (about 60 g/2 oz.)
½ raw beetroot/beet (about 80 g/3 oz.)
35 g/⅓ cup ground flaxseeds
grated zest of 1 organic orange
1 tablespoon freshly squeezed orange juice
2 tablespoons freshly snipped chives
¼ teaspoon ground turmeric
¼ teaspoon ground coriander
2 tablespoons tahini (or toasted, ground sesame seeds)

1 tablespoon olive oil (if using ground sesame seeds instead of tahini)
1 teaspoon umeboshi vinegar (optional)
salt, to taste
1 tablespoon raw sesame seeds, for sprinkling

dehydrator lined with a tex-flex sheet (or a baking sheet lined with baking parchment)

MAKES 16 SMALL FALAFELS

In a food processor fitted with an 'S' blade, separately chop the sunflower seeds (you want a slightly chunky consistency), then the carrots with the beetroot/beet. Mix together in a bowl, then add the ground flaxseeds, orange zest and juice, chives, spices, tahini/ground sesame and oil (if using) and combine all the ingredients (except for the raw sesame seeds for sprinkling) into a compact paste.

Form 16 small balls with moist hands, then flatten them slightly. Sprinkle the top of each falafel with raw sesame seeds, and place on the lined dehydrator or baking sheet.

Dehydrate on 60°C (140°F) for 1 hour, lower to 45°C (115°F) and continue dehydrating until the falafels form a crust, with a still slightly moist inside (takes 4–5 additional hours). (Alternatively, use the oven: Turn it to the lowest setting, and put in the baking sheet with falafels, wedging the door open with a rolled-up dish towel to prevent overheating.)

MEALS

If you've never baked chickpeas/garbanzo beans in the oven, I urge you to give this recipe a try! This quick and easy dish lets you enjoy the flavours of falafel, without the hassle of deep-frying or the mess of rolling into balls.

LUSCIOUS UNDONE FALAFEL SALAD

**FOR THE CHICKPEAS/
GARBANZO BEANS**

2 tablespoons tamari soy
  sauce
¼ teaspoon chilli/chili
  powder
¼ teaspoon ground
  turmeric
¼ teaspoon ground ginger
½ teaspoon ground
  coriander
¼ teaspoon ground cumin
1 tablespoon olive oil
160 g/1 cup cooked
  chickpeas/garbanzo
  beans, well drained

FOR THE SALAD

20 g/1 cup rocket/arugula
1 round/butterhead
  lettuce (about
  160 g/5½ oz.)
6 leaves red leaf lettuce
2 ripe tomatoes (about
  340 g/¾ lb.)
1 small bunch fresh basil
1 portion Mediterranean
  Seed Falafel mixture
  (do not form into
  falafels, see page 35)
2 tablespoons olive oil
2 tablespoons red wine
  vinegar
1 portion Tzatziki Sauce
  (see page 61)
4 pitta pockets, cut into
  wedges, toasted,
  to serve

*baking sheet, lined with
baking parchment*

SERVES 2-4

Preheat the oven to 180°C (350°F) Gas 4.

For the chickpeas/garbanzo beans, mix together all the ingredients apart from the chickpeas/garbanzo beans to make a marinade. Pour the marinade over the chickpeas/garbanzo beans and toss to coat well.

Spread the coated chickpeas/garbanzo beans on the lined baking sheet and bake in the preheated oven until the chickpeas/garbanzo beans soak in all the marinade and start browning. Alternatively, you could do this in a frying pan/skillet: Heat the pan, add the chickpeas/garbanzo beans, pour over the marinade and mix quickly with two wooden spoons over high heat until fragrant and well roasted.

Wash the salad leaves well and drain. Tear the lettuce leaves into smaller pieces. Cut the tomatoes into wedges and chop the basil. Place all the vegetables in a big wide bowl, crumble over the Mediterranean falafel mixture, add the baked chickpeas/garbanzo beans and drizzle with olive oil and vinegar. Mix well to incorporate.

Divide into separate plates and serve the tzatziki sauce in 2–4 small bowls, so each person can pour it over the falafel salad just before eating.

There's nothing quite like biting into a big, juicy falafel burger! A cast-iron pan/skillet is essential for frying these – it means they need very little oil but won't stick to the pan. It also uniquely gives the delicious charred flavour.

PERFECTLY CHARRED FALAFEL BURGERS

260 g/1½ cups cooked chickpeas/garbanzo beans, well drained
130 g/¾ cup very finely grated beetroot/beets
130 g/1 cup pre-soaked couscous (pour 120 ml/ ½ cup boiling water over 65 g/½ cup couscous, add a little salt, cover and let sit for 10 minutes)
70 g/½ cup good-quality bread crumbs

2 tablespoons tahini
3 tablespoons finely chopped onion
2 garlic cloves, crushed
¾ teaspoon salt
½ teaspoon dried thyme
½ teaspoon dried oregano
freshly ground black pepper
sunflower or coconut oil, for frying

SERVING SUGGESTION
6 whole-wheat burger buns
Roasted Red Pepper and Mustard Sauce (see page 57)
lettuce leaves
Tofu Mayonnaise (see page 53)
slices of fresh onion
pickles and wooden barbecue sticks
Super Simple Salsa (see page 54)

MAKES 6 BIG BURGERS

In a food processor fitted with an 'S' blade, pulse the chickpeas/garbanzo beans. Transfer to a mixing bowl and add all the remaining ingredients, except the frying oil. Use your hands to knead the mixture thoroughly; everything should be well incorporated. Chill in the fridge for 20 minutes, or longer.

Form the mixture into 6 patties. I usually use a big cookie cutter or an American ½ cup measuring cup for one burger – slightly oil the inside to prevent sticking, fill the cup and turn it over onto a baking sheet. Pat down to make a nicely shaped burger.

Preheat a cast-iron pan/skillet over medium heat. Pour in 1 tablespoon of oil and add two–three burgers (more if your pan is bigger). Fry for about 5 minutes each side, adding a tablespoon more oil after the flip. Cook until the burgers are heated through, slightly charred and have a thin crust.

This is my serving suggestion for a real burger experience: while the pan is still hot, fry the inside of a whole-wheat bun, spread the bottom part with red pepper and mustard sauce, add lettuce leaves, top with the burger, spread tofu mayo on top, add slices of fresh onion and top with the bun. Pierce with a wooden barbecue stick and add a couple of pickles. Serve with super simple salsa!

I don't often use store-bought vegan cheese in my kitchen, but this recipe is an exception – it's hard to resist the melted cheese in comforting casserole-style dishes! This is something different which everybody will enjoy.

HEAT-AND-EAT FALAFEL CASSEROLE

FOR THE TOMATO SAUCE

3 tablespoons extra virgin olive oil

1 large onion (about 120 g/4 oz.), finely chopped

1 teaspoon vegetable bouillon powder or ½ bouillon cube (optional)

1 teaspoon dried oregano or basil

1 tablespoon rice, agave or maple syrup

1 tablespoon tamari soy sauce

230 ml/1 cup tomato passata

2 garlic cloves, crushed

2 tablespoons freshly chopped parsley or snipped chives

salt and freshly ground black pepper, to taste

MAKES ABOUT 375 ML/1½ CUPS SAUCE

230 ml/1 cup tomato sauce (see left)

7–9 leftover falafel (choose any from the recipes in this cookbook)

50 g/½ cup grated white Cheddar-style vegan cheese that melts well (such as Cheezly)

olive oil, to drizzle

blanched broccoli or any other greens, to serve

toasted sourdough bread or creamy mashed potatoes, to serve

large baking dish

SERVES 2-3

Start by making the tomato sauce. Heat the olive oil in a pan over medium heat and sauté the onion until translucent. Add the bouillon powder/cube, herbs, syrup and tamari, and stir until the onion soaks up the spices; about 2 minutes.

Add the passata and bring it to the boil. Now lower the heat and leave to simmer, uncovered, for about 10 minutes, or until thick. At the very end of cooking, add the garlic, parsley or chives and an extra drop of olive oil. Season to taste. This sauce can be made a couple of days in advance and kept refrigerated, if needed.

To assemble the casserole, preheat the oven to 180°C (350°F) Gas 4.

Drizzle a little bit of olive oil in the bottom of the baking dish, pour in the tomato sauce, add a layer of leftover falafel and cover with grated vegan cheese. Bake for 10–15 minutes, until the tomato sauce starts sizzling and the cheese melts. Serve with blanched broccoli or any other greens, toasted sourdough bread or creamy mashed potatoes.

This is a great way to use up those leftover falafels sitting in the fridge! Since traditional falafels usually contain coriander, they go well with Indian curry spices. Chickpea patties also add satisfying texture, and transform a light vegetable curry into a heartier and more filling meal.

FALAFEL COCONUT CURRY

2 tablespoons virgin coconut oil
1 large onion (about 120 g/4½ oz.), finely chopped
1 carrot (about 70 g/ 2½ oz.), chopped into bite-sized pieces
1 celery stalk/rib (about 70 g/2½ oz.), chopped
2-cm/¾-inch piece of fresh ginger, peeled and finely chopped
2 garlic cloves, chopped
1½ tablespoons mild curry powder
2 teaspoons ground ginger
2 teaspoons ground turmeric
2 teaspoons garam masala
¼ teaspoon chilli/chili powder, or to taste
2 tablespoons tamari soy sauce

500 ml/2 cups coconut milk (home-made or from carton, not full-fat canned milk)
½ teaspoon salt
Leftover Traditional Chickpea Falafels (see page 11) or Red Lentil Falafels (see page 15)
1 tablespoon kuzu, arrowroot or cornflour/ cornstarch, diluted in a little cold water
chopped spring onions/ scallions or coriander/ cilantro, to garnish
basmati rice, chapatis or toasted pitta pockets, to serve

SERVES 4

Heat the coconut oil in a pan and sauté the onion, carrot and celery with a pinch of salt, until fragrant. Add the ginger, garlic and dry spices, combine and let fry for another minute. Add the soy sauce and stir. Add enough coconut milk to cover the vegetables and bring to the boil, then add the salt, lower the heat and simmer until the vegetables are soft. Add more coconut milk if necessary.

At the end of cooking, add the leftover falafel and diluted thickener of choice (if needed), and let the curry come to the boil one last time. Adjust the seasoning to taste. Garnish with chopped spring onions/scallions or coriander/cilantro and serve with basmati rice, chapatis or toasted pitta pockets.

SAUCES AND DIPS

CASHEW 'YOGURT' SAUCE

If you love yogurt-based sauces, but are avoiding dairy and soy, then here's a great alternative! Cashews are mild in taste and can be used as a base in many delicious recipes, especially those mimicking yogurt or cream cheese dishes.

180 g/1⅓ cups cashews
4 tablespoons freshly
    squeezed lemon juice,
    or to taste
1 teaspoon agave syrup
    (optional)

MAKES ABOUT 400 ML/1²/₃ CUPS

Put the cashews in a bowl, cover with water and let soak for 24 hours. Drain, discarding the soaking water and rinse well.

Blend the soaked cashews with the rest of the ingredients and 175 ml/¾ cup cold water in a high-speed blender until silky smooth. Keep refrigerated and use within 2 days.

TOFU MAYONNAISE

A vegan version of popular mayonnaise that is much lighter and much less oily than regular mayo, or even the store-bought vegan mayo. This pairs up very well with any fried or baked falafel.

300 g/2 cups fresh tofu
60 ml/¼ cup olive or
    sunflower oil
3 tablespoons freshly
    squeezed lemon juice
    or apple cider vinegar
1 soft date
½ teaspoon sea salt

MAKES ABOUT 240 ML/1 CUP

Blend all the ingredients together with 6 tablespoons water until completely smooth. Taste and adjust the seasonings. I like it tangier so I always add a little more lemon juice or vinegar. Also, pay attention to what you will serve it with; if used as a salad dressing, it needs to be more sour, and if used with salty foods like falafel, make it less salty.

HERB AND AVOCADO DIP

Apart from using avocado for guacamole, sliced in salads or adding it to salsas, it can be blended into a creamy dip that goes well with most things.

1 ripe avocado (about 250 g/9 oz.), peeled and stoned/pitted
4 tablespoons olive oil
1 tablespoon tahini paste
1 tablespoon freshly squeezed lemon juice
1 teaspoon tamari soy sauce
¼ teaspoon Cayenne pepper, or to taste
1 bunch fresh herbs (basil, coriander/cilantro, parsley, lemon balm/melissa)
coconut milk or water, as needed
salt, to taste

MAKES ABOUT 240 ML/1 CUP

Place the avocado in a blender or food processor, add all the other ingredients and blend until smooth, adding coconut milk or water until the desired consistency. Taste and adjust the seasoning.

You can use any nut/seed butter instead of tahini – peanut butter, for example, is an interesting choice. You can make endless variations of this dip/sauce by adding garlic, onion or vinegar – all depending on what you have in the pantry. Lemon juice postpones the browning process of the avocado, but even so, it's best used the same day.

SUPER SIMPLE SALSA

With fried foods such as falafel, it's very important to serve raw vegetables alongside to add nutrition. This easy salsa tastes even better the next day!

3 ripe tomatoes (about 550 g/1¼ lbs.), stems removed
handful of fresh basil leaves
3 tablespoons finely chopped onion
1 garlic clove, finely chopped
3 tablespoons extra virgin olive oil
¼ teaspoon dried oregano
sea salt, to taste
freshly ground black pepper, to taste

MAKES ABOUT 700 ML/3 CUPS

Slice the tomatoes in half and remove the juice and the seeds. Dice the flesh and place in a serving bowl. Tear the basil leaves by hand and add them to the tomatoes together with all the other ingredients. Mix well and let sit for at least half an hour to allow the flavours to combine.

The best variety of peppers to use for this yummy sauce are long, red pointed Romano peppers, but if you can't find them you can use red (bell) peppers too. Roasting peppers deepens their flavour and gives a wonderful aroma, and goes well with any kind of falafel.

ROASTED RED PEPPER AND MUSTARD SAUCE

1 kg/2¼ lbs. Romano peppers
60 ml/¼ cup extra-virgin olive oil
2 tablespoons smooth Dijon mustard
4 garlic cloves, crushed
apple cider vinegar, to taste
chilli/chili powder or freshly ground black pepper (optional)
sea salt, to taste

baking sheet, lined with baking parchment

MAKES ABOUT 240 ML/1 CUP

Preheat the oven to 180°C (350°F) Gas 4.

Wash and pat-dry the peppers, leaving them whole. Place the whole peppers on the baking sheet and roast in the preheated oven for 20–25 minutes, turning frequently until the entire pepper skin has turned black and blistery.

Remove from the oven, put the peppers into an airtight container and let rest, tightly covered for long enough to build up the steam; about 15 minutes. This will make peeling the skin easier.

Save all the liquid that leaks from the peppers while cooling, and the liquid coming out as you peel and deseed.

Blend the peeled and deseeded peppers in a blender or food processor until smooth, adding the oil, collected juices, Dijon mustard, garlic, salt and a little vinegar. You can also add a little chilli/chili powder or black pepper, for extra heat. Add more pepper juice or oil to reach the desired consistency. Store in a tightly covered sterilized jar in the fridge and use within 1 month.

Buying tahini paste is really easy and there are lots of good-quality brands out there, but there's just something very satisfactory in making it at home, from scratch. It's definitely cheaper, too. You just need to invest a bit of time and energy in it, and owning a high-speed blender is really helpful if you want it to turn out oily and creamy, as it should be.

TAHINI SAUCE

4 tablespoons tahini paste
(see below)
1 garlic clove, crushed
1 tablespoon freshly
snipped chives
freshly squeezed lemon
juice, to taste
about 120 ml/½ cup oat,
rice or almond milk
salt and freshly ground
black pepper

FOR THE TAHINI PASTE
450 g/3 cups unhulled
sesame seeds
¼ teaspoon salt

MAKES ABOUT 150 ML/⅔ CUP

Start by making the tahini paste. Place the sesame seeds in a very fine-mesh sieve/strainer and wash thoroughly under running water. Do not skip this step, as the sesame seeds will toast much more evenly and washing them prevents them from jumping out of the pan. Drain really well.

Put the sesame seeds in a cast-iron frying pan/skillet over medium heat. Roast in two batches, if the whole amount doesn't fit in the frying pan/skillet at once. Dry-roast the seeds, stirring constantly until the seeds turn golden brown and start puffing up and cracking. Check if they are done by placing a couple of seeds between your fingers – if the seeds crumble easily, they are ready.

Blend the seeds in a high-speed blender with the salt, pushing them down from the sides with the tamper while blending. After a couple of minutes, the ground sesame seeds will start turning into a creamy tahini! Spoon out into a sterilized dry jar, let cool and keep tightly covered.

To make the tahini sauce, mix together the tahini paste, garlic, chives, lemon juice and a little salt and freshly ground black pepper, adding just enough milk to get a smooth sauce. Refrigerate any leftovers for later use.

Here's my version of the famous tzatziki dip that is served in every taverna bar on every Greek island, and it's so popular with both natives and tourists!

TZATZIKI SAUCE

2 cucumbers
   (about 400 g/14 oz.),
   peeled and grated
500 ml/2 cups soy yogurt
6 tablespoons extra virgin
   olive oil
1 tablespoon umeboshi
   vinegar (optional)
2 garlic cloves, crushed
freshly squeezed lemon
   juice, to taste
1 tablespoon freshly
   chopped parsley leaves
1 tablespoon freshly
   snipped chives
salt

MAKES ABOUT 700 ML/3 CUPS

Mix the grated cucumbers with a little salt and let sit for 15 minutes. Squeeze out as much of the cucumber juice as you can, otherwise the liquid will water down the dip.

Mix all other ingredients in a bowl and add the cucumber flesh. Chill until ready to serve.

There you have it! It's the most refreshing snack and it's on my menu every week from the beginning to the end of the cucumber season. A great dip to serve with Greek-style Falafel (see page 23), but actually, you can also serve it with any other falafel in this cookbook!

INDEX

A

arugula *see* rocket
avocado: herb and avocado
  dip 54

B

baked falafels 26–33
basil
  herb and avocado dip 54
  luscious undone falafel
    salad 45
  Mediterranean seed
    falafel 35
BBQ falafel croquettes 27
beetroot
  perfectly charred falafel
    burgers 46
  pink sun-seeds falafel 43
bell peppers *see* peppers
broad beans: fresh broad
  bean falafel 12
brown lentils: falafel
  'meatballs' 31
buckwheat and cauliflower
  bites 36
burgers, perfectly charred
  falafel 46

C

carrots
  falafel coconut curry 50
  falafel 'meatballs' 31
  juicy brown rice faux-lafel
    32
  pink sun-seeds falafel 43
cashews
  cashew yogurt sauce 53
  paprika and cashew
    falafel 40

casserole, heat-and-eat
  falafel 49
cauliflower: buckwheat and
  cauliflower bites 36
celeriac
  falafel 'meatballs' 31
  juicy brown rice faux-lafel
    32
chard: red lentil falafel
  wraps 15
cheese: heat-and-eat falafel
  casserole 49
chickpea flour and harissa
  patties 19
chickpeas
  fennel and lemon-scented
    falafel 16
  luscious undone falafel
    salad 45
  perfectly charred falafel
    burgers 46
  traditional chickpea
    falafel pockets 11
chives
  buckwheat and
    cauliflower bites 36
  pink sun-seeds falafel 43
  tahini sauce 58
chunky baked falafel patties
  28
cilantro *see* coriander
coconut milk: falafel
  coconut curry 50
coriander
  crunchy tofu faux-lafel 24
  herb and avocado dip 54
  robust tempeh faux-lafel
    20
courgettes

Greek-style falafel fritters
  23
mushroom and walnut
  falafel 39
couscous: perfectly charred
  falafel burgers 46
croquettes, BBQ falafel 27
crunchy tofu faux-lafel 24
cucumbers: tzatziki sauce 61
curry, falafel coconut 50

D

dips
  herb and avocado dip 54
  super simple salsa 54

F

falafel coconut curry 50
falafel 'meatballs' 31
fava beans *see* broad beans
fennel and lemon-scented
  falafel 16
flaxseeds
  mushroom and walnut
    falafel 39
  pink sun-seeds falafel 43
fried falafels 10–25
fritters, Greek-style falafel 23

G

garbanzo beans *see* chickpeas
gluten-free
  BBQ falafel croquettes 27
  buckwheat and
    cauliflower bites 36
  cashew yogurt sauce 53
  chickpea flour and harissa
    patties 19
  crunchy tofu faux-lafel 24
  falafel coconut curry 50
  fresh broad bean falafel 12

heat-and-eat falafel
  casserole 49
herb and avocado dip 54
juicy brown rice faux-lafel
  32
luscious undone falafel
  salad 45
Mediterranean seed
  falafel 35
mushroom and walnut
  falafel 39
paprika and cashew
  falafel 40
pink sun-seeds falafel 43
roasted red pepper and
  mustard sauce 57
robust tempeh faux-lafel 20
super simple salsa 54
tahini sauce 58
tofu mayonnaise 53
tzatziki sauce 61
Greek-style falafel fritters 23
green lentils: falafel
  'meatballs' 31

H

harissa: chickpea flour and
  harissa patties 19
heat-and-eat falafel
  casserole 49
herb and avocado dip 54

J

juicy brown rice faux-lafel 32

K

kidney beans: chunky baked
  falafel patties 28

L

lemon balm: herb and
  avocado dip 54

lemons: fennel and lemon-scented falafel 16
lentils
    falafel 'meatballs' 31
    red lentil falafel wraps 15
lettuce: luscious undone falafel salad 45

M
mayonnaise, tofu 53
meals 44–51
'meatballs', falafel 31
Mediterranean seed falafel 35
millet: BBQ falafel croquettes 27
mint: fresh broad bean falafel 12
mushroom and walnut falafel 39
mustard: roasted red pepper and mustard sauce 57

O
oats: falafel 'meatballs' 31
olives: crunchy tofu faux-lafel 24

P
paprika and cashew falafel 40
parsley
    fresh broad bean falafel 12
    Greek-style falafel fritters 23
    herb and avocado dip 54
    Mediterranean seed falafel 35
    paprika and cashew falafel 40
    robust tempeh faux-lafel 20

patties
    chickpea flour and harissa patties 19
    chunky baked falafel patties 28
peppers
    paprika and cashew falafel 40
    roasted red pepper and mustard sauce 57
    robust tempeh faux-lafel 20
    perfectly charred falafel burgers 46
pink sun-seeds falafel 43
pitta pockets
    fennel and lemon-scented falafel 16
    luscious undone falafel salad 45
    traditional chickpea falafel pockets 11
polenta: BBQ falafel croquettes 27
pumpkin seeds: Mediterranean seed falafel 35

R
raw falafels 34–43
red kidney beans: chunky baked falafel patties 28
red lentil falafel wraps 15
rice: juicy brown rice faux-lafel 32
robust tempeh faux-lafel 20
rocket: luscious undone falafel salad 45
Romano peppers: roasted red pepper and mustard sauce 57

S
salad, luscious undone falafel 45
salsa, super simple 54
sauces
    cashew yogurt sauce 53
    roasted red pepper and mustard sauce 57
    tahini sauce 58
    tofu mayonnaise 53
    tzatziki sauce 61
seeds
    Mediterranean seed falafel 35
    pink sun-seeds falafel 43
sesame seeds
    chunky baked falafel patties 28
    tahini sauce 58
shiitake mushrooms: mushroom and walnut falafel 39
soy yogurt: tzatziki sauce 61
spinach: red lentil falafel wraps 15
sun-dried tomatoes
    buckwheat and cauliflower bites 36
    Mediterranean seed falafel 35
sunflower seeds
    Mediterranean seed falafel 35
    pink sun-seeds falafel 43
super simple salsa 54

T
tahini
    herb and avocado dip 54
    perfectly charred falafel burgers 46

pink sun-seeds falafel 43
    tahini sauce 58
tempeh: robust tempeh faux-lafel 20
tofu
    crunchy tofu faux-lafel 24
    juicy brown rice faux-lafel 32
    tofu mayonnaise 53
tomatoes
    buckwheat and cauliflower bites 36
    heat-and-eat falafel casserole 49
    luscious undone falafel salad 45
    Mediterranean seed falafel 35
    super simple salsa 54
tortillas: red lentil falafel wraps 15
tzatziki sauce 61

W
walnuts
    Mediterranean seed falafel 35
    mushroom and walnut falafel 39
wraps, red lentil falafel 15

Y
yogurt
    cashew yogurt sauce 53
    tzatziki sauce 61

Z
zucchini see courgettes

COOK'S NOTES

- Both British (Metric) and American (Imperial plus US cups) measurements are included in these recipes for your convenience; however, it is important to work with one set of measurements and not alternate between the two within a recipe.
- All spoon measurements are level unless otherwise specified.
- Ovens should be preheated to the specified temperatures. We recommend using an oven thermometer. If using a fan-assisted oven, adjust temperatures according to the manufacturer's instructions.
- When a recipe calls for the grated zest of citrus fruit, buy unwaxed fruit and wash well before using. If you can only find treated fruit, scrub well in warm soapy water before using.